ARES

APEX

BY CHRISTINE HA

WWW.APEXEDITIONS.COM

Apex is distributed by North Star Editions:
sales@northstareditions.com | 888-417-0195

Produced for Apex by Red Line Editorial.

Photographs ©: Shutterstock Images, cover, 1, 10–11, 12, 14–15, 16–17, 19, 22–23, 24–25, 26–27; iStockphoto, 4–5, 6–7, 8–9, 13, 18, 20–21, 29

Library of Congress Control Number: 2020952910

ISBN
978-1-63738-012-3 (hardcover)
978-1-63738-048-2 (paperback)
978-1-63738-118-2 (ebook pdf)
978-1-63738-084-0 (hosted ebook)

Printed in the United States of America
Mankato, MN
082021

NOTE TO PARENTS AND EDUCATORS

Apex books are designed to build literacy skills in striving readers. Exciting, high-interest content attracts and holds readers' attention. The text is carefully leveled to allow students to achieve success quickly. Additional features, such as bolded glossary words for difficult terms, help build comprehension.

TABLE OF CONTENTS

CHAPTER 1

FIERCE FIGHTER 5

CHAPTER 2

GOD OF WAR 11

CHAPTER 3

ARES AND ATHENA 17

CHAPTER 4

NOT POPULAR 23

Comprehension Questions • 28

Glossary • 30

To Learn More • 31

About the Author • 31

Index • 32

FIERCE FIGHTER

Swords clanged against shields. Spears flew through the air. Soldiers dodged fierce blows. Ares fought along with them. It was **chaos**, and he loved it.

The god Ares enjoyed causing fights.

Ares rode through the battle on his **chariot**. His horses weaved between soldiers. The men fought harder when he passed. Their shouts grew louder.

Greek soldiers often rode chariots into battle.

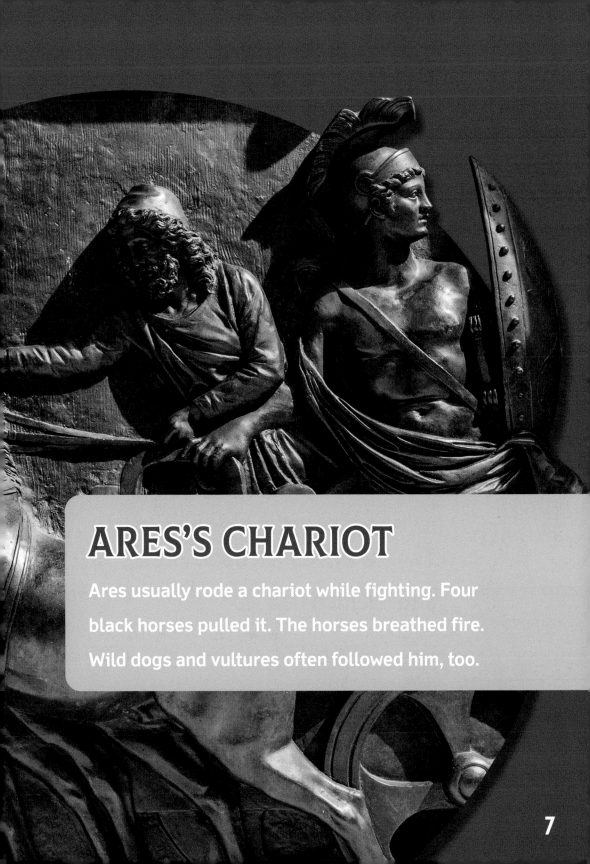

ARES'S CHARIOT

Ares usually rode a chariot while fighting. Four black horses pulled it. The horses breathed fire. Wild dogs and vultures often followed him, too.

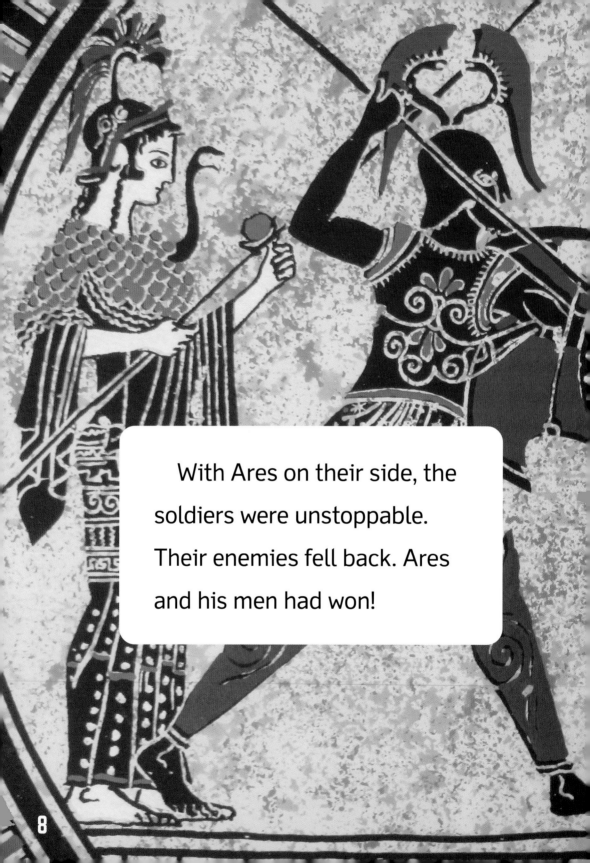

With Ares on their side, the soldiers were unstoppable. Their enemies fell back. Ares and his men had won!

Greek soldiers carried round shields.

Ares usually fought with a spear and a shield. Sometimes he also had a sword.

9

CHAPTER 2

GOD OF WAR

Ares was the god of war. He was the son of Zeus and Hera. Many stories say he was born in northeastern Greece.

Legends say Ares was born in Thrace. The land in this area was wild.

Ares was **violent**. He got angry quickly. He often started fights and battles.

Some Greek soldiers wore helmets with tall crests on the tops.

In art, Ares is often shown wearing a helmet.

The name Ares comes from the Greek word are. It means "curse" or "ruin."

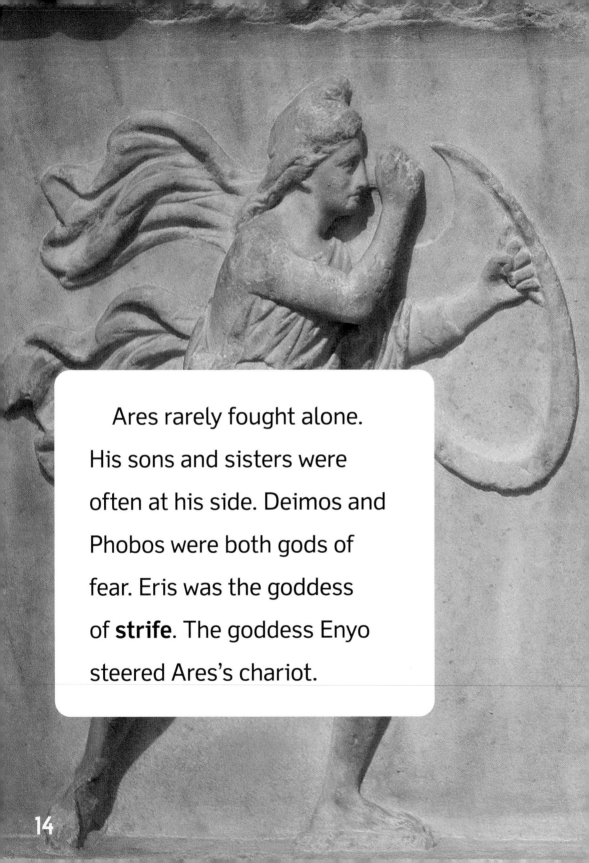

Ares rarely fought alone. His sons and sisters were often at his side. Deimos and Phobos were both gods of fear. Eris was the goddess of **strife**. The goddess Enyo steered Ares's chariot.

The Amazons fought several famous battles against Greek armies.

THE AMAZONS

In Greek myths, the Amazons were a tribe of **warrior** women. They were known for their courage. They rode horses well, too. Legends say they were daughters of Ares.

CHAPTER 3

ARES AND ATHENA

A res had great strength. But people sometimes beat him. They got help from the goddess Athena. She could outsmart Ares.

Athena was the goddess of wisdom. She often helped people win battles.

Athena often helped heroes fight Ares. For example, Ares tried to kill Hercules. But Athena kept the hero safe. He fought Ares and won.

In Greek myths, heroes often fought gods and monsters.

Ares and Athena helped opposite sides in the Trojan War. Athena's side won.

Athena helped the Greeks trick the Trojans. Soldiers hid inside a giant horse.

DIFFERENT STRENGTHS

Ares and Athena were both gods of war. They controlled different parts of fighting. Ares liked force and violence. Athena focused on **strategy** and skill.

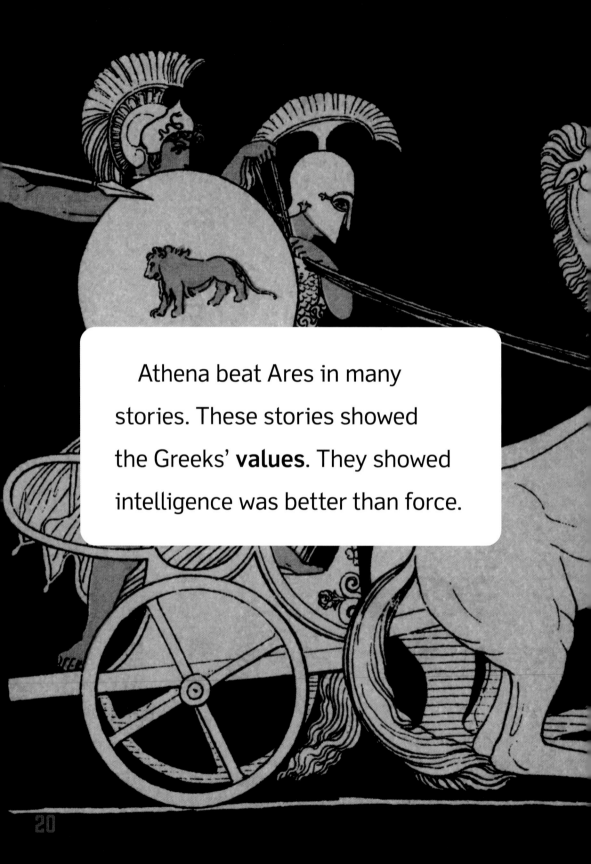

Athena beat Ares in many stories. These stories showed the Greeks' **values**. They showed intelligence was better than force.

CHAPTER 4

NOT POPULAR

Many Greeks didn't like Ares. He was often angry. And he was **destructive**. These traits made him unpopular. Few people prayed to him.

The Roman god Mars was much more popular than the Greek god Ares.

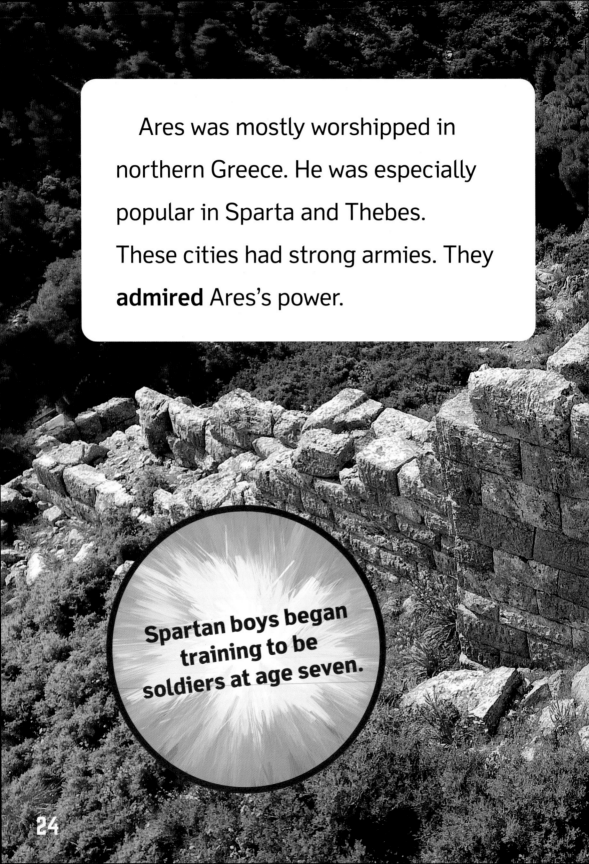

Ares was mostly worshipped in northern Greece. He was especially popular in Sparta and Thebes. These cities had strong armies. They **admired** Ares's power.

Spartan boys began training to be soldiers at age seven.

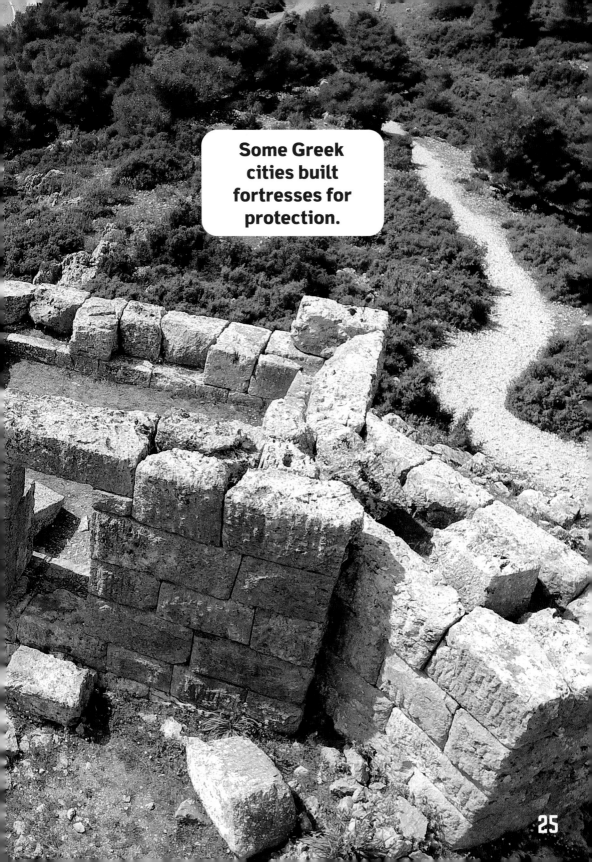

Some Greek cities built fortresses for protection.

25

One temple for Ares stood in the city of Athens.

Ares did have a few temples. They often stood outside of cities. People placed them there for protection. They thought Ares would stop enemies from getting in.

TRAPPED

In one story, two giants captured Ares. They trapped him in a bronze pot. They kept him there for more than a year. His battles had ruined their **crops**.

COMPREHENSION QUESTIONS

Write your answers on a separate piece of paper.

1. Write a few sentences explaining the main ideas of Chapter 4.

2. Would you want Ares to be on your side in a fight? Why or why not?

3. Which goddess did Ares often fight against?

    A. Eris

    B. Enyo

    C. Athena

4. How were the Amazons similar to Ares?

    A. They were skilled fighters.

    B. They were calm and peaceful.

    C. They were sons of Zeus.

5. What does **weaved** mean in this book?

*His horses **weaved** between soldiers. The men fought harder when he passed.*

    A. stayed in one place

    B. twisted and turned while moving

    C. made thread into fabric

6. What does **captured** mean in this book?

*In one story, two giants **captured** Ares. They trapped him in a bronze pot.*

    A. caught someone

    B. lost someone

    C. let someone go

Answer key on page 32.

GLOSSARY

admired
Liked or wanted to be like someone or something.

chaos
Total lack of order, often because things are messy or loud.

chariot
A two-wheeled cart pulled by horses or other animals.

crops
Plants that people grow for food.

destructive
Causing lots of damage.

strategy
Careful planning to solve a problem or reach a goal.

strife
Feelings or fights that are bitter and angry.

values
Beliefs about what is good or important.

violent
Likely to use physical force to hurt or attack.

warrior
A brave person who has fought many battles.

TO LEARN MORE

BOOKS

Abdo, Kenny. *Spartans*. Minneapolis: Abdo Publishing, 2020.

Buckey, A. W. *Greek Gods, Heroes, and Mythology*. Minneapolis: Abdo Publishing, 2019.

Temple, Teri. *Ares: God of War*. Mankato, MN: The Child's World, 2019.

ONLINE RESOURCES

Visit **www.apexeditions.com** to find links and resources related to this title.

ABOUT THE AUTHOR

Christine Ha lives in Minnesota. She enjoys reading and learning about myths and legends from around the world.

INDEX

A
Amazons, 15
Athena, 17–20

C
chariot, 6–7, 14

D
Deimos, 14

E
Enyo, 14
Eris, 14

G
giants, 27

H
Hera, 11
Hercules, 18
heroes, 18

M
Mars, 21

P
Phobos, 14

S
shields, 5, 9
Sparta, 24
spears, 5, 9
swords, 5, 9

T
temples, 27
Thebes, 24
Trojan War, 19

Z
Zeus, 11

Answer Key:
1. Answers will vary; **2.** Answers will vary; **3.** C; **4.** A; **5.** B; **6.** A